Charles Yeld

The life of devotion

Parts I. and II. of the introduction to a devout life

Charles Yeld

The life of devotion

Parts I. and II. of the introduction to a devout life

ISBN/EAN: 9783742857712

Manufactured in Europe, USA, Canada, Australia, Japa

Cover: Foto ©Lupo / pixelio.de

Manufactured and distributed by brebook publishing software (www.brebook.com)

Charles Yeld

The life of devotion

THE LIFE OF DEVOTION;

Being Parts I. and II. of the

INTRODUCTION TO A DEVOUT LIFE:

FROM THE FRENCH OF

S. FRANÇOIS DE SALES,

Bishop and Prince of Geneva.

For the use of Members of the English Church.

TRANSLATED AND EDITED

BY THE

REV. CHARLES YELD, B.A.,

*Curate of S. Matthew's,
One of the Masters of the High School,*

LONDON:
William Skeffington, 163 Piccadilly.

1869.

THE AUTHOR'S PRAYER OF DEDICATION.

O SWEET JESUS, my LORD, my SAVIOUR, my GOD, Behold me prostrate before Thy Majesty, devoting and consecrating this work to Thy Glory; Give life by Thy blessing to its words, that those souls for whom I have written it, may receive from it the sacred inspiration which I desire for them. Especially that they may implore for me Thine Infinite Mercy; to the end that, while I show to others the way of Devotion in this world, I myself be not rejected and cast away in the world to come; but that, with them, I may for ever sing, as my Song of Triumph, the words which with my whole heart I utter now, amidst the hazards of this mortal life;

LIVE JESUS, LIVE JESUS: YEA, LORD JESUS, LIVE AND REIGN IN OUR HEARTS FOR EVER AND EVER. AMEN.

EDITOR'S PREFACE.

S. François de Sales, the "eminent Saint and Servant of God,[*] who by preaching, life, directing of souls, and by his writings, has won and is still winning his thousands to the love of God," began his ministry in the Roman Communion, in the year 1591. He was of noble birth but of nobler disposition, as he showed in the devout and loving spirit which marked him from his earliest years, and which is breathed in every page of the "Vie Dévote." The scene of his early work, and indeed of the work of his whole life, was Chablais and the neighbourhood of Geneva; and there the bright rays of his sanctity, the lustre of his zeal for God's Honour, his love of peace, his compassion for the poor, and above all the purity and simplicity of his life, won for him a name and praise in the earth, and gained the esteem and reverence even of the bitterest opposers of his Church— of the very men whose influence he was appointed to counteract. At the age of 57, after a ministry of more than

[*] Preface (E. B. P.) to "The Spiritual Combat." London: Parkers and Rivingtons, 1868.

thirty years, he went Home, S. John the Evangelist's Day, 1622.

In the Preface to his work, he describes the object he had in view in writing it. Hitherto, he says, devotion had been treated of as proper only to those living wholly retired from the world, and his aim was to show that as, "near the Chelidonian Islands springs of fresh water are found in the midst of the sea, and as the firefly lives in the flames without singeing its wings," so a resolute soul may live in the world without being injured by any of its follies and vanities, may find sweet springs of piety amidst the world's salt waters, may fly amid the flames of earthly affection without burning the wings of the holy desires of a devout life. And this object he has certainly attained. The "Vie Dévote" is one of those rare books, in which one finds reduced to art the very inmost principles of a devout and holy life: its loving counsels are suited to every condition, its rules and precepts have Church-wide reference and are all plain and easy to be understood. It ranks by the side of the Spiritual Combat, the Imitation of CHRIST and our own Bishop Taylor's Holy Living; but it is written with an originality and quaintness of style which are most pleasing and which one does not meet with in any other book. The numberless editions in the French through which it has passed, witness the value which the members of his own Communion have attached to it; but these rather increase the work of a translator. The exuberance of thought has found new expression and new phraseology with each new editor, and I have seen no two editions quite alike; it has thus been a matter of some little difficulty to ascertain S. François' own words. In translating I have allowed myself such license as will generally, I hope, be considered just. I have endeavoured to give strictly my Author's meaning, altering only such parts as were contrary to the teaching of our own Branch of the Church. Happily these necessary changes I have found to be very few. As S. François said of the Spiritual Combat, so may it be said of his "Vie Dévote," it is clear, concise, and "all practical;" there has therefore been little to vary or omit.

My first intention was to publish a translation of the whole five Parts together; but the two here offered form so excellent a manual of devotion, are so complete in themselves and so distinct from the rest, that I have yielded to the wish of friends, and send forth these first; hoping to add at some future day the remaining three Parts, which contain Advice upon the Practice of the Virtues, and Aids to resist Temptation and to encourage Devotion.

If by God's favour this little volume gain admittance into any home, therein to give bent to an aimless life, or divert into a holier channel the absorbing devotion of thought to business or pleasure, or any other worldly occupation, I shall be more than satisfied. I would take as my own the words of S. François:* "It is true, dear reader, that I here write of a devout life, without being myself devout, yet certainly not without a desire of becoming so; and it is this affection towards it which encourages me to instruct thee. For as a great and learned man has said, 'To hear is a good way to learn, to study is still better, but to teach is the best of all.' . . . . . The fair and chaste Rebecca, watering Isaac's camels was destined to be his wife, and received from him ear-rings and bracelets of gold. Thus do I hope, through the Infinite Goodness of GOD, that in conducting his dear sheep to the wholesome waters of devotion, He will make my soul His spouse, putting in my ears the golden words of His Holy Love, and on my arms the strength to practise good works; which I humbly beseech His Majesty to grant to me and to all the children of His Church."

C. Y.

NOTTINGHAM,
    Sexagesima, 1869.

* Preface to the "Vie Dévote."

CONTENTS.

PART I.

CHAPTER.	PAGE.
I. TRUE DEVOTION DESCRIBED	1
II. THE EXCELLENCE OF DEVOTION	5
III. DEVOTION SUITED TO ALL CONDITIONS	8
IV. THE BEGINNING OF HOLINESS IS TO BE CLEANSED FROM SIN	10
V. WE MUST STRIVE AGAINST THE AFFECTION TO SIN	13
VI. HOW THE AFFECTION TO SIN MAY BEST BE ROOTED OUT	15
VII. THE FIRST MEDITATION. ON OUR CREATION	16
VIII. THE SECOND MEDITATION. ON THE END FOR WHICH WE WERE CREATED	20
IX. THE THIRD MEDITATION. ON THE BENEFITS OF GOD	24
X. THE FOURTH MEDITATION. ON SIN	28
XI. THE FIFTH MEDITATION. ON DEATH	32
XII. THE SIXTH MEDITATION. ON PARADISE	35
XIII. A PROTESTATION TO ENGRAVE IN THE SOUL A FIRM RESOLUTION TO SERVE GOD	39
XIV. WE MUST CLEANSE OURSELVES FROM THE AFFECTION TO VENIAL SINS	42
XV. OF UNPROFITABLE AMUSEMENTS	43
XVI. ON REGULATING OUR NATURAL INCLINATIONS	45

PART II.

CHAPTER.	PAGE
I. Of the Necessity of Prayer	48
II. A brief Method of Meditation; and first of the Presence of God, which is the first point of Preparation	51
III. Of Invocation, the second point of the Preparation	55
IV. Of the third point of Preparation, which consists in proposing the subject of the Mystery whereon we mean to meditate	56
V. Of Considerations, which form the second part of the Meditation	58
VI. Of Affections and Resolutions; the third part of the Meditation	59
VII. Of the Conclusion, and the Spiritual Bouquet	60
VIII. Useful Advice upon the practice of Meditation	62
IX. Of the dryness which we sometimes feel in Meditation	66
X. Of the Morning Exercise	68
XI. Of the Evening Exercise and Examination of Conscience	70
XII. Of the Spiritual Retreat	72
XIII. Of Aspirations, Ejaculatory Prayers and Good Thoughts	75
XIV. How we ought to hear and read the Word of God	78
XV. Of Frequent Communion	79
XVI. How we ought to Communicate	83

PART THE FIRST.

CHAPTER I.

True Devotion described.

You aspire to lead a life of devotion, because as a Christian your religion teaches you that such a life is well-pleasing to God. But as the little faults we begin with, grow with our growth, and are at last almost irreparable, it is above all necessary that you should know what devotion really is; for there is but one true devotion, while there are many vain and false, and without rightly distinguishing which is the true, you may become attached to a devotion both superstitious and imprudent. The painter Arellius represented in his pictures those to whom he was attached; and thus it is that each one paints devotion according to his own fancy. Those who practise fasting believe themselves to be devout if they fast often, although they may cherish bitterness in their hearts; and whilst they dare not dip the end of their tongue in wine, lest they sin, they do not fear to employ that same tongue in destroying the reputation of a neighbour by slander and calumny. Another esteems himself devout, because he says daily a long series of prayers, although he may afterwards utter grievous, proud and injurious words. One draws alms freely from his purse to give to the poor, though he cannot draw gentleness from his heart to forgive his enemies; another pardons his enemies but will not pay his creditors, unless forced by justice. All these persons pass for devout, but are really not so by any means.

True and living devotion pre-supposes the love of GOD; or rather it is itself no other thing than a true love of GOD; this love, in that it adorns the soul and makes us acceptable with GOD, is called Grace; in that it gives us power to do good, it is called Charity; but when, come to perfection, it gives us the will not only to do good, but to work constantly, carefully, promptly, then it is called Devotion. This is explained by a natural and simple comparison. The ostrich has wings but never flies; fowls fly seldom, and always low and heavily; but eagles, doves and swallows are lofty, rapid and constant in their flight. Thus sinners fly not towards GOD, but ever on and for the earth; the good, as yet imperfect, fly up to GOD in well-doing, but slowly and heavily; it is only souls really devout who rise to Him by a rapid, lofty and constant flight. In a word Devotion is nothing else but the spiritual activity and ardour by which Charity acts in us, and we by her, with promptness and affection; and as it belongs to Love to make us observe the Commandments of GOD, so it is the part of Devotion to lead us to keep these with all diligence and fervour. He who observes not all God's Commandments can be esteemed neither righteous nor devout; for to be righteous one must have charity, and to be devout one must have, in addition to charity, great zeal and earnestness in doing charitable actions. And because devotion consists in the perfection of love, not only does it render us prompt, active, and diligent in the observance of all GOD's commands, but it excites us to perform, with loving energy, every good work. For as a man newly recovered from some sickness, walks only as much as is necessary, and that slowly and wearily; so a sinner, just healed of his iniquity, walks in the way which GOD commands, but wearily and slowly, until he has caught the spirit of piety, and then like a man strong and healthy, he does not walk only, but runs and leaps forward in the paths of GOD and in the way of His heavenly precepts.

Lastly, love and devotion are not more different one from the other, than the fire from its flame; seeing that love is the spiritual fire of the soul which, when kindled to a bright glow, is called devotion. So that devotion adds nothing to the fire of love save the flame which renders it ready, active and diligent in the observance of the commands and precepts of GOD.

CHAPTER II.

The Excellence of Devotion.

THEY who discouraged the Israelites from entering the Land of Promise told them that the land devoured its inhabitants; by which they meant that the air was so malignant that none could live long therein, and that, moreover, the natives were such monsters as to prey upon men as grasshoppers (Numbers xiii. 33). Thus it is that the world condemns devotion; describing religious persons as of sad and morose countenance, and declaring that devotion begets a temperament at once melancholy and unsociable. But as Joshua and Caleb protested that not only was the Promised Land "an exceeding good land" (Numbers xiv. 7), but that the possession of it would be pleasant and delightful, so does the HOLY SPIRIT by the mouth of all His saints, and Our LORD by His own Mouth, assure us that the life of devotion is one of pure pleasure and happiness.

The world sees that devout persons fast, pray, suffer

injuries, tend the sick, give to the poor, watch, repress their anger, stifle their passions, and accomplish other actions which in their nature are painful and rigorous; but the world sees not the inward devotion and earnestness which render all such acts pleasant and easy. Look at bees upon the thyme; they find a bitter juice, which in sucking they change to honey. Thus the devout may find bitterness in mortification, but in its exercise it is changed for them to sweetness. The fire of martyrdom, the flame, the rack, the sword seemed but as flowers and perfume, transformed by a martyr's love. If devotion could give sweetness to the most cruel torments, even to death itself, what shall it not do to the practice of virtue? Sugar, we know, sweetens unripe fruits, and corrects the often hurtful acid of those that are ripe; thus devotion is the true spiritual sweetness which takes from mortifications their bitterness and from human consolations their danger; it lightens the hardships of the poor and represses the eagerness of the rich; it consoles the sorrow and desolation of the oppressed, and humbles the pride of the prosperous; it charms the weariness of solitude and moderates the enjoyments of those who are in the world; it is to our souls as fire in winter, as flowers in summer; it knows how "to abound and to suffer need;" it renders equally useful honour and contempt; it receives with the same disposition pleasure and grief, and fills us with a marvellous sweetness.

Contemplate the ladder which Jacob saw, for it is a faithful picture of a devout life; the two sides represent prayer which asks the love of GOD, and the Sacraments which confer it; the steps are the different degrees of love, by which one passes from grace to grace, either in descending by act to succour and support our neighbour, or in rising by contemplation to loving union with GOD. Observe those who are on the ladder; they are men with Angels' hearts, or Angels with human bodies; they are not young, though they seem so, for they are full of vigour and spiritual activity; they have wings to fly and spring upward to GOD in holy prayer, but they have feet to walk with men in saintly life and conversation; while the serene beauty of their countenance speaks of the gentle tranquillity with which all events are received by them.

Believe me, devotion is the sweet of sweets, the queen of virtues, the perfection of love; for it is to love what the flower is to the plant, lustre to the precious stone, and scent to the costly balm—the odour of sweetness which comforts the spirits of men and rejoices Angels.

CHAPTER III.

Devotion suited to all Conditions.

GOD in creating the world commanded the trees to bear fruit, each after his kind. Thus He commands all Christians, who are the living trees of His Church, to produce worthy fruits of devotion according to their station and calling. Devotion should be practised differently by the gentleman, by the mechanic, by the servant, by the prince, by the widow, the child, the married woman; and not only so, it must be suited to the health, the business and the duties of each. Would it be right for a Bishop to lead a retired life, or for an artizan to be all day long engaged in the offices of the Church? Would not this be wrong—inconsistent with the position of either? Yet these, or similar mistakes do occur often; and the world which does not, or will not discern between devotion and the indiscretion of those who would be thought devout, murmurs at and blames devotion for faults in which it has no share.

No; devotion, when it is right and true, injures nothing; it is false when it becomes an obstacle to the legitimate duties of our calling. "The bee," says Aristotle, "gathers honey from the flowers, without injury to them, leaving them as fresh and perfect as she finds them." True devotion does yet better; it not only hinders no good work in the world, but on the contrary helps forward and brightens all. By it the care of the family is rendered less burdensome, the love of husband and wife more sincere, the service of the prince more faithful, and every occupation of life more pleasant.

It is an error, even a heresy, to wish to banish the devout life from the palace of the prince, from the shop of the artizan, from the homes of the married, from the camp of the army. True, that devotion purely contemplative is in many conditions impracticable; there is, however, devotion of another character to bring to perfection those who live in the world. Abraham, Isaac and Jacob, David and Job, Sarah and Rebecca, are illustrious examples in the Old Testament; and in the New, Joseph and Lydia were devout in their shops; Martha, Aquila and Priscilla in their households; the centurion Cornelius in the army. It has even happened that some have in solitude fallen from the perfection they had attained in the world. Wherever we are, whatever be our calling, we can and we ought to aspire to the perfect life.

CHAPTER IV.

The beginning of Holiness is to be cleansed from Sin.

WHEN "the flowers appear on the earth," we are told,* it is time to prune the trees. What are the flowers of our

* Compare Canticle ii. 12.

heart but good desires? and when these make themselves felt, the heart must be purified from all dead works, must put off the old man and put on the new, in forsaking sin, and casting away whatever may turn it from the love of GOD. The commencement of holiness is to be cleansed from sinful lusts. In S. Paul this cleansing was effected perfectly and in a moment; but a like healing is as great a miracle in the order of grace as the resurrection of the dead in that of nature. Healing, as of the body, so of the soul, is wrought little by little, step by step, not without much time and labour.

The Angels, on the ladder which Jacob saw, had wings but did not fly, mounting up to Heaven step by step. The soul rising from sin to the life of devotion is compared to the dawn of morning which drives away the darkness, not instantly but by degrees. "The cure which is made slowly," says the proverb, "is ever the most sure." The diseases of the soul, like those of the body, come posting on horseback, but depart slowly on foot. One must be armed with courage and patience in entering the path of devotion. Alas! how sad is it to see some, who knowing themselves to be subject to numberless imperfections, (after having a little exercised themselves in devotion) begin to be troubled and discouraged almost at the outset, and even yield to the temptation to go back and forsake all. But on the other hand, is it not a temptation fraught with extreme danger, for a soul to believe itself healed of all imperfections from the first day of its conversion, to deem itself perfect before having attained to anything of holiness, to attempt to fly without wings?

The endeavour to purify the soul cannot, nor ought to, end but with our life. Let us not then be troubled at the sight of our failings, for our perfection consists in vanquishing these; and can we meet and fight with them without seeing them? can we vanquish without meeting them? Our victory lies not in not feeling, but in not consenting to them.

But to be disturbed by them—this is not to consent to them: nay, it is well, for the exercise of our humility, that in this spiritual combat we be sometimes wounded. We are never conquered but when we lose life or heart. Let a blessed condition for us in this spiritual warfare, that we can always conquer, if we will always fight.

CHAPTER V.

We must strive against the Affection to Sin.

ALL the Israelites went out of Egypt, but all did not go out in heart and affection; so that many regretted in the desert the fleshpots of Egypt. Thus there are penitents who leave the state of sin, but do not relinquish their affection for it; that is, they purpose to sin no more, but it is with reluctance of heart to deprive themselves of the pleasures of sin: their heart renounces sin and avoids it, yet slips back to its very verge through wistful looks at the forsaken evil, as of old Lot's wife looked back to Sodom. They abstain from sin, as sick men do from melons, which they do not actually eat because their doctor threatens them with death if they do eat; but they are troubled under this privation; they talk of them and are unwilling to believe them hurtful; they would at least smell them and think those happy who may eat them. Thus do weak and fainthearted penitents abstain from sin, but with reluctance; they would willingly sin and not be damned; they speak of sin with relish, and esteem those happy who give themselves up to it. A man, in a moment of contrition, abandons his design to revenge himself; but soon after one will find him among his friends, speaking with pleasure of his quarrel, and saying, *Had it not been for the fear of God he would have done this or that: how strict is God's Law on this point! Would to God he had been permitted to revenge himself!* Who does not see that though this poor man is free from actual sin, yet his heart is tied and bound by affection for it: he is out of Egypt, it is true, but in desire he has returned thither, yearning for its coarse dainties—the fleshpots which were erst his food.

Alas! in how great danger of perdition are such penitents!

Since you are willing to enter upon the devout life you must not only forsake sin itself, but also cleanse your heart from all affection to sin. For, besides the danger of relapsing, these miserable passions waste and deject your spirit, and deprive your good works of the zeal and perseverance and cheerful earnestness which are the essence of devotion.

CHAPTER VI.

How the Affection to Sin may best be rooted out.

THE first means to be employed in attaining this purification of the soul, consists in forming a strong and vivid idea of all the evil sin has caused in the world and in feeling deep and earnest contrition. For if contrition however feeble, so it be *real*, purifies the heart from sin, when it is great and profound, it cleanseth us from all the affections which depend on sin.

Our contrition therefore must be deep and earnest, that it may extend to the least circumstances of sin. David, in his penitence, protested that he not only abhorred sin, but also all the ways and paths of it. In this consists the renewing of the soul, which is compared by the same Prophet to the renewing of the eagle. (Psalm ciii. 5. Comp. Isaiah xl. 31.)

To arrive at this contrition—this fear of sin, you must practise carefully the following meditations, the using of which will, by the help of God's grace, root out of your heart sin and its affection. To this end I have prepared them. You will use them in order, taking but one for each day, and that if possible in the morning, which is the most proper time for spiritual exercises; to the end that you may think over and meditate on them throughout the day. But if you are not yet accustomed to meditation, have recourse to that which will be said in the Second Part.

CHAPTER VII.

The first Meditation. On our Creation.

PREPARATION.

Place yourself in thought in the Presence of God. Beseech Him to inspire you.

CONSIDERATIONS.

1. Consider that only a few short years ago you were not yet in the world, and that your existence was as

nothing. Where were we, O my soul, at that time? The world had already lasted long, and had no need of us.

2. Think how GOD has taken you out of this nothingness to make you what you are, only of His goodness; having no need at all of you.

3. Consider the being that GOD has given you, for it is the highest in the visible world; it is created for eternal life and is capable of being perfectly united with His Divine Majesty.

AFFECTIONS AND RESOLUTIONS.

1. *Humble yourself deeply before God.* Say from your heart, with the Psalmist, O LORD, I am as nothing in Thy sight;* how hast Thou thought upon me to create me? Alas, my soul, thou wert lost in this nothingness, and hadst been there still, had GOD not drawn thee thence.

2. *Give thanks to God.* O my Great and Good CREATOR, how much do I owe to Thee, for having brought me into being, and made me by Thy Mercy what I am. What can I do to bless Thy Holy Name, and to thank Thee for Thy vast goodness.

* Comp. Psalm xxxix. 5.

3. *Abase yourself.* But alas! my CREATOR, instead of uniting myself to Thee, by love and service, I am become rebellious through my unruly affections; wandering and straying from Thee, and yielding myself to sin; not honouring Thy Goodness more than if Thou hadst not been my CREATOR.

4. *Prostrate yourself before God.* O my soul, know that the LORD is thy GOD; it is He that hath made thee, not thou thyself. O GOD, I am the work of Thy Hands. I will no longer take pleasure in myself, since of myself I am nothing. Why dost thou magnify thyself, O dust and ashes? Why dost thou exalt thyself? I will humble myself, will act, and suffer: I will change my life, henceforth follow my CREATOR, and esteem myself honoured with the being He has given me, consecrating it wholly to the obedience I owe to Him according to the means which shall be granted me, and in which I shall be instructed.

CONCLUSION.

1. *Thank God.* Bless the LORD, O my soul, and all that is within me praise His Holy Name; for His Good-

ness has drawn me out of nothing and His Mercy has created me.

2. *Offer yourself.* O my GOD, I offer to Thee all that Thou hast given me, from my heart to Thee I dedicate and consecrate all.

3. *Pray.* O my GOD, strengthen me in these affections and resolutions, and with me all for whom I desire to pray.

Our FATHER, Which art in Heaven, Hallowed be Thy Name. Thy kingdom come. Thy will be done in earth, As it is in Heaven. Give us this day our daily bread. And forgive us our trespasses, As we forgive them that trespass against us. And lead us not into temptation; But deliver us from evil: For Thine is the kingdom, The power, and the glory, For ever and ever. Amen.

After your prayer, make, as it were, a spiritual bouquet of the considerations which have most moved your spirit and touched your heart. You can then think them over from time to time in the course of the day, to sustain you in your good resolutions.

CHAPTER VIII.

The Second Meditation. On the end for which we are created.

PREPARATION.

Place youself in thought in the Presence of GOD.
Pray Him to inspire you.

CONSIDERATIONS.

1. It is not through any need of us that GOD created us, since we are altogether unprofitable to Him; but only that He may in us exercise His Goodness, and raise us by His Grace to be partakers of His Glory. To that end He has enriched us with an understanding to know and adore Him, a memory to be mindful of Him, a heart to love Him, an imagination to conceive His benefits, eyes to behold His wondrous works, a tongue to praise Him— and so of the other faculties.

2. Created for this intention, it behoves you to condemn and avoid all actions which are contrary to it, and to despise as vain and frivolous whatever does not fall in with the purposes of GOD.

3. Consider the wretchedness of the world which thinks

The Life of Devotion. 21

not of this—the misery of those who live as though they believed themselves created to no other end than to build houses, plant trees, heap up riches, and spend their days in folly.

AFFECTIONS AND RESOLUTIONS.

1. *Abase yourself, reproaching your soul with its misery in having so long forgotten these truths.* Alas! How was my spirit engaged, O my GOD, when I thought not of Thee? What were my memories, when I forgot Thee? What did I love, when I loved not Thee? I ought to have nourished myself upon truth, and I feasted upon vanity. Slave of the world, I served it, which was made to serve me and to teach me to know and glorify Thee.

2. *Strive to hate your past life.* I renounce you then, false maxims, vain thoughts, hateful memories! I hate you, false and faithless friendships, vain attachments to the world, lost services, miserable pleasures!

3. *Return to God.* And Thou, O my GOD, my SAVIOUR, Thou shalt henceforth be the sole object of my thoughts. Never-more will I think upon that which is displeasing to Thee. My memory shall ever dwell upon the greatness of

Thy mercy to me; Thou shalt be the delight of my heart, the joy of my affections.

Ah! the many vanities which engrossed my mind, the many trifles which squandered my time, the many affections which enchained my heart—these shall be henceforth hateful to me: and I will employ all means to make them ever the more hateful.

CONCLUSION.

1. *Thank God, who created you for so excellent an end.* I give thanks to Thee, O my GOD, who hast created me for Thyself, and for the eternal enjoyment of Thine incomprehensible Glory. Oh, when shall I be worthy of it? when praise Thee as I ought?

2. *Make your offering to Him.* I offer to Thee, O most loving CREATOR, these affections and resolutions with all my heart and with all my soul.

3. *Pray.* I beseech Thee, O my GOD, to accept these my desires and vows, to give Thy Holy Benediction to my soul, to the end that It may strengthen me to fulfil them, through the merits of the blood of Thy dear Son, shed for me upon the Cross.

Our FATHER, Which art in Heaven, Hallowed be Thy Name. Thy kingdom come. Thy will be done in earth, As it is in Heaven. Give us this day our daily bread. And forgive us our trespasses, As we forgive them that trespass against us. And lead us not into temptation; But deliver us from evil: For Thine is the kingdom, The power, and the glory, For ever and ever. Amen.

I believe in GOD the FATHER Almighty, Maker of Heaven and Earth. And in JESUS CHRIST, His only SON our LORD, Who was conceived by the HOLY GHOST, Born of the Virgin Mary, Suffered under Pontius Pilate, Was Crucified, Dead, and Buried, He descended into Hell; The third day He rose again from the dead, He ascended into Heaven, And sitteth on the right hand of GOD the FATHER Almighty, from thence He shall come to judge the quick and the dead.

I believe in the HOLY GHOST, the Holy Catholic Church, the Communion of Saints, the Forgiveness of sins, the Resurrection of the body, and the Life Everlasting. Amen.

(Make here your bouquet of devotion.)

CHAPTER IX.

The Third Meditation. On the Benefits of God.

PREPARATION.

Place yourself in thought in the Presence of GOD.

Pray Him to inspire you.

CONSIDERATIONS.

1. Consider the corporal graces which GOD has bestowed upon you; what a body, with a conformation so perfect and with all necessary means of maintaining it; what health and lawful recreations to cheer it; what natural pleasures attached to your station—the help and assistance of your inferiors, the pleasant and agreeable society of your friends. Think of all this in comparison with the lot of others much more worthy than yourself, who are deprived of these advantages; some with deformed bodies, maimed limbs, ill health; others abandoned by friends, covered with reproach, contempt, dishonour, oppressed with poverty and sickness. And GOD has not willed that you should be thus miserable.

2. Consider your gifts of mind. See how many in the world are stupid, senseless, passionate, mad; brought up in grossness and ignorance. Is it not GOD, Who has specially watched over you, in giving you a happy disposition and a good education?

3. Consider above all your spiritual gifts. You are a child of the Catholic Church. GOD has taught you to know Him, even from your youth. How has He given to you His Sacraments! How many inspirations of Grace, of inward light; how many reproaches of conscience for your amendment! How frequently has He pardoned your faults, and watched to deliver you lest you should cast yourself away, and your soul be lost eternally! And were not these years past given you as a time and opportunity to advance the good of your soul? Think well over each of these favours, and see how good and gracious GOD has been to you.

AFFECTIONS AND RESOLUTIONS.

1. *Admire the Goodness of God.* O, how good is my GOD to me! O, how gracious is He! How rich is Thy

heart, O LORD, in pity; how great in mercy! O my soul, let us rehearse for ever the goodness of the LORD, and tell out His works with gladness.

2. *Repent of your ingratitude.* But what am I, O LORD, that Thou art so mindful of me! Oh, how great is my unworthiness! Alas, I have even trodden under foot Thy blessings. I have dishonoured Thy goodness; I have opposed the depth of my ingratitude to the unfathomable depth of Thy Grace and Mercy.

3. *Rouse yourself to acknowledgment.* O my heart, be no more unfaithful, ungrateful, disloyal to this great Benefactor. How shall not my soul be henceforth wholly subject to GOD Who has wrought so many wonders and graces in me and for me?

Withdraw then your heart from pleasures and train it to bear the yoke of the service of CHRIST. Apply your soul to know and acknowledge Him by such exercises as may be most suitable. Avail yourself of the means of salvation which GOD has given you in His Church. Yes, O my GOD, I will seek Thee in prayer and praise; I will frequent the Holy Sacrament, will hear Thy Holy Word, will obey

Thy voice in putting into practice Thy counsels and inspirations.

CONCLUSION.

1. Thank GOD for the knowledge He has given you of His benefits and your duties.

2. Offer to Him your heart with all your resolutions.

3. Pray Him that He will strengthen you, and give you faithfulness to perform His will, through the merits of the death of His Son, JESUS CHRIST.

Our FATHER, Which art in Heaven, Hallowed be Thy Name. Thy kingdom come. Thy will be done in earth, As it is in Heaven. Give us this day our daily bread. And forgive us our trespasses, As we forgive them that trespass against us. And lead us not into temptation; But deliver us from evil: For Thine is the kingdom, The power, and the glory, For ever and ever. Amen.

(Make here your spiritual bouquet.)

CHAPTER X.

The fourth Meditation.   On Sin.

PREPARATION.

Place yourself in thought in the Presence of God. Beseech Him to inspire you.

CONSIDERATIONS.

1. Call to mind how long it is since you began to sin, and examine how much, since that beginning, sins have been multiplied in your heart; how every day you have increased them against God, against yourself, against your neighbour, by word, by deed, by thought and desire.

2. Consider your evil inclinations, and how far you have followed them; and by these two points you will see that your faults are more than the hairs of your head in number —even as many as the sand of the sea.

3. In particular, call seriously to mind the sin of ingratitude to God, which overshadows all the rest. Think how many benefits God has bestowed upon you, and how you

have abused them to His dishonour; especially how many inspirations you have despised, how many good impulses you have rendered useless. But more than all, how often have you received the Holy Sacrament, and where are the fruits thereof? What is become of all those precious jewels wherewith The Beloved adorned your soul? All buried under your iniquities! Think of this ingratitude, that when GOD so sought you out to save you, you fled away from Him to destruction.

AFFECTIONS AND RESOLUTIONS.

1. *Humble yourself in your misery.* O my GOD, how dare I appear before Thee? Alas! I am but the corruption of the world, a well of iniquity and ingratitude. Can it be that I have carried my disloyalty so far? that there is not one of my senses, not one of the powers of my soul, which I have not injured, profaned and sullied? not one day of my life that has not borne ill fruit? Is this the use I should have made of the benefits of my CREATOR, and the precious Blood of my REDEEMER?

2. *Ask pardon and cast yourself at the Feet of your Lord,*

like a prodigal child. Have mercy, LORD, on me a sinner. O Living Fountain of compassion, have pity on me in my misery.

3. *Resolve to live better.* O LORD, by the help of Thy Grace, never again will I give myself to Sin. Alas! I have loved it too well. Now I detest it, and embrace Thee, O Father of Mercies. I would live and die in Thee.

4. To efface these sins past I will bravely accuse myself of them, and not leave one unbanished from my heart.

5. I will do all I can to root sin out of my heart; will embrace constantly the means provided for me, never feeling that I have done enough to repair such grievous offences.

CONCLUSION.

1. Thank GOD who has waited even to this hour for your conversion, and has given you these affections.

2. Offer to Him your heart, that you may act up to your good resolutions.

3. Pray Him to strengthen you and to grant you His protection and favour.

The Life of Devotion.

Our FATHER, Which art in Heaven, Hallowed be Thy Name. Thy kingdom come. Thy will be done in earth, As it is in Heaven. Give us this day our daily bread. And forgive us our trespasses, As we forgive them that trespass against us. And lead us not into temptation; But deliver us from evil: For Thine is the kingdom, The power and the glory, For ever and ever. Amen.

I believe in GOD the FATHER Almighty, Maker of Heaven and Earth. And in JESUS CHRIST, His only SON our LORD, Who was conceived by the HOLY GHOST, born of the Virgin Mary, Suffered under Pontius Pilate, Was Crucified, Dead, and Buried, He descended into Hell; The third day He rose again from the dead, He ascended into Heaven, And sitteth on the right hand of GOD the FATHER Almighty, from thence He shall come to judge the quick and the dead.

I believe in the HOLY GHOST, the Holy Catholic Church, the Communion of Saints, the Forgiveness of sins, the Resurrection of the body and the Life Everlasting. Amen.

(Make your spiritual bouquet).

CHAPTER XI.

The fifth Meditation.   On Death.

PREPARATION.

Place yourself in thought in the Presence of GOD.
Ask His Grace.
Imagine yourself to be very ill, on the point of death, and without hope of recovery.

CONSIDERATIONS.

1. Consider the uncertainty of the day of your death. O my soul thou must one day quit this body. When shall that time be? Shall it be in winter or summer, by day or by night? Shall it be suddenly or with warning? by illness or by accident? Shall I have time to confess my sins and to receive the help of my spiritual pastor? . Alas! of all this we know nothing; only certain is it that we shall die, and always sooner than we expect.

2. Consider that when the world shall end for you—for to you *it* will then die—it will all be changed before your

eyes; yes, then the pleasures, the vanities, the worldly joys, the fond affections of our lives, will seem but as shadows, and clouds of air. Ah! for what trifles and idle fancies have I offended my GOD! *Then* will you see that you have forsaken Him for nothing; while on the contrary devotion and good works will seem pleasant and delightful; and why, you will ask, did I not follow this beautiful and happy path? Then sins, which before appeared but small, will be great—as mountains, and your devotion small indeed.

3. Consider the sorrowful—the long farewell your soul will then take of the world; she will say adieu to riches, vanities, idle companions; to kindred, children, husband, wife; in short to everything which this world holds, and last of all to her own body, which she will leave dismantled and corrupting.

4. Consider with what haste your body will be hidden under the earth; and that done, the world will have no further memory of you, even as you have lost thought of others who are gone. "GOD give him peace" they will

say, and that is all. O death, how pitiless, how ruthless art thou!

5. Consider how the soul shall wing its flight to GOD'S Right Hand—or His Left! Ah, whither shall yours go? What way shall it take? No other, be assured, than that it began to walk in here on earth.

AFFECTIONS AND RESOLUTIONS.

1. *Pray to the Father of Mercies, and cast yourself into His Arms.* Receive me, O my LORD, into Thy protection on that dreadful day; make that hour happy and favourable for me, and let all the other days of my life be sad and sorrowful.

2. *Despise the world.* Seeing that I know not the hour in which I must leave thee, O world, I will no more fix my love on thee. And you O friends beloved, may my affection for you be only such holy love as shall endure for ever; may no bonds bind us which death must break or dissolve.

3. I would prepare myself for that last hour, take all possible care to end my life's journey happily.

CONCLUSION.

Give thanks to GOD for these resolutions which He has given you. Offer them to His Divine Majesty. Beseech Him to grant you a happy death, through the merits of the death of His dear SON.

Our FATHER, Which art in Heaven, Hallowed be Thy Name. Thy kingdom come. Thy will be done in earth, As it is in Heaven. Give us this day our daily bread. And forgive us our trespasses, As we forgive them that trespass against us. And lead us not into temptation; But deliver us from evil: for Thine is the kingdom, The power, and the glory, For ever and ever. Amen.

(Make a bouquet of myrrh.)

CHAPTER XII.

The Sixth Meditation.   On Paradise.

PREPARATION.

Place yourself in thought in the Presence of GOD. Beseech Him to inspire you by His Grace.

CONSIDERATIONS.

1. Picture to yourself a clear, beautiful night and think how pleasant it is to gaze upon the sky brilliant with the fires of so many stars; and then imagine this beauty joined to that of a lovely day in such a manner that the brightness of the sun dims not the lustre of the stars and moon. Remember that all this loveliness is as nothing, compared with the excellent glory of Paradise. O, how precious, how fair, is the Holy City of GOD.

2. Consider the nobleness, the beauty, the excellence of the holy society of those who dwell there: the millions of millions of Angels, of Cherubim and Seraphim; the multitude, which no man can number, of Apostles, Prophets, Martyrs, Confessors, Virgins, holy Matrons—the number cannot be told. O blessed union of the Saints in the glory of their GOD. The meanest of them all is far more beautiful to behold than the whole world; what will it be to see them all! How happy too are they! Singing evermore the wondrous melody of eternal love, joying in the rapture of heavenly happiness, they live in the unspeakable con-

tentments of a society that knows neither sorrow nor partings.

3. Consider finally the happiness they enjoy in looking upon God, Who there blesses them for ever with His loving regard, flooding their hearts with a torrent of love and heavenly delight. How great a happiness is it to be united everlastingly with their Maker. They are like happy birds singing perpetually in the air of His Divinity which encompasses them on all sides with inconceivable joys. Unceasingly they sing the praises of their Creator's love. "Blessed be Thou for ever O our sweet and sovereign Creator and Saviour, Who art so bountiful to us and dost bestow upon us so lavishly the treasures of Thy Glory." He too blesses them. "Blessed be ye for ever, My beloved children, who with so great love and courage have served Me and will praise Me throughout eternity."

AFFECTIONS AND RESOLUTIONS.

1. *Admire and praise this Celestial Country.* How beautiful art thou, O dear Jerusalem; how happy are they who dwell within thy walls.

2. *Reproach your heart with its little courage in being so easily turned from the path to this glorious abode.* Why have I so far strayed from my sovereign good? Wretch that I am! for these foolish and trifling pleasures have I a thousand times forsaken eternal and infinite delights! Was I mad, to despise such precious blessings for vain and miserable fancies?

3. *Aspire with fervour to this blissful habitation.* O my GOD, since it has pleased Thee at length to direct my wandering steps into the right way, never hereafter will I turn back. Onward, my soul, to this infinite repose; onward to this blessed Land which is promised to us. What do we in this Egypt? I will not be hindered by anything that would deter me from the road or stay me in it.

Whatever can lead or urge me on, this I will gladly do.

CONCLUSION.

Thank GOD for giving you these good resolutions. Offer them to Him with all your heart.

Pray Him to lead you on daily in the steps of His most holy life.

Our FATHER, Which art in Heaven, Hallowed be Thy Name. Thy kingdom come. Thy will be done on earth, As it is in Heaven. Give us this day our daily bread. And forgive us our trespasses, As we forgive them that trespass against us. And lead us not into temptation; But deliver us from evil: For Thine is the kingdom, The power, and the glory, For ever and ever. Amen.

(Do not forget to make a spiritual bouquet.)

CHAPTER XIII.

Protestation to engrave in the soul a firm resolution to serve God.

I NOW in the Presence of the Eternal GOD, having considered the exceeding mercy of His Divine goodness to me, unworthy and sinful creature, whom he has created out of nothing, has preserved, sustained, delivered from so many dangers and filled with so many benefits; but, above all, having considered the incomprehensible sweetness and clemency wherewith this most good GOD has so graciously spared me in my iniquities, so often inspired me with a wish to amend and so patiently waited for my repentance even to this day of my life, notwithstanding all my ingratitude, and the unfaithfulness with which, deferring my conversion and despising His grace, I have so rashly offended Him. Having moreover considered that on the day of my holy Baptism I was so happily given and dedicated to my GOD, to be His child, and that contrary to the profession then made for me, I have so many times miserably and hatefully profaned my mind by employing it against His Divine Majesty—now returning to myself, prostrate in heart and mind before the Throne of Divine Justice, I acknowledge and confess myself guilty of the death and passion of my LORD JESUS CHRIST, by reason of the sins which I have committed and for which He suffered the torments of the cross, the agony of a shameful death. I acknowledge that I justly deserve to be cast away for ever.

But turning to the Throne of the infinite Mercy of the same eternal GOD; detesting with all my heart and all my strength the iniquities of my past life, I humbly crave pardon, grace and mercy, with absolution from my offences, by virtue of the death and passion of the same LORD and REDEEMER of my soul; upon Whom relying, as the only Foundation of my hope, I renew the sacred profession of allegiance made for me at my Baptism, renouncing the devil, the world and the flesh, detesting their evil suggestions and lusts, now and evermore.

And turning to my GOD, gracious and full of compassion, I desire, purpose and resolve, irrevocably to serve and love Him henceforth for ever; dedicating and consecrating to Him my mind, with all its faculties; my soul, with all its powers; my heart, with all its affections; my body, with all its senses; protesting never more to abuse any part of my being against His Divine Will and Sovereign Majesty: to Whom I offer up and sacrifice myself in spirit, to be a loyal, obedient and faithful creature, all the days of my life.

But if, alas! by the suggestion of my enemy, or through human frailty, I transgress this my vow and resolution, I protest and determine from this hour that by the assistance of the HOLY GHOST I will rise again as soon as I shall perceive my fall and will return anew to the Divine Mercy.

This is my wish, my intention, my resolution, which I here ratify and confirm in the Sacred Presence of my GOD and of His Church.

May it please Thee, O my eternal GOD, All-powerful and All-good, FATHER, SON and HOLY GHOST, to confirm in me this resolution, and to accept this my sacrifice: And as thou hast given me the will, so grant me power and grace to perform it. O GOD Thou art my GOD—GOD of my heart, GOD of my soul, GOD of my spirit. Thus would I acknowledge and adore Thee now and throughout eternity. Live, LORD JESUS.

CHAPTER XIV.

We must cleanse ourselves from the affection to venial sins.

As the daylight increases, we see more clearly in the glass the spots and blemishes of our face; even so as the inward light of the HOLY GHOST more and more illumines our conscience, we see more plainly and distinctly the sins and imperfections which hinder us from attaining to true

The Life of Devotion.

devotion. The same light which shows us our spiritual spots and stains, inflames us likewise with a desire to be cleansed from them.

You will discover then that besides mortal sins and the affection for them (from which you have prayed for deliverance) there remain in your soul divers inclinations to venial sins, and from these it is necessary that you should be purified. Venial sin, be it ever so little, displeases GOD; though not so highly that He will reject or condemn us for it; it is as the dead fly, which, says the Wise Man, mars the sweetness of an ointment; if it get a lodgment in the soul, it mars, nay it destroys, devotion; for it cannot be that a devout heart should take pleasure in doing anything which is displeasing to GOD.

CHAPTER XV.

Of unprofitable Amusements.

AMUSEMENTS, feasts, dress, outward show, comedies, are not in their nature evil; they are indifferent, and may be used both well and ill; yet they are dangerous, and to bear affection for them is more dangerous. I say then, that though it be lawful to dance, to adorn oneself, to be present at honest comedies, to banquet; yet to be over fond of such things is contrary to devotion and very dangerous.

It is no sin to do such things; it is a sin to pursue them immoderately or irregularly. It is wrong to sow in the garden of our heart such vain and foolish affections, which take up the room of virtuous and holy impressions, and hinder the sap of our souls from nourishing good desires and inclinations. The ancient Nazarites abstained not only from all wine and strong drinks, but also from grapes, lest tasting the grape they might be tempted to drink the wine. I deny not that we may sometimes enjoy amusements such as I have mentioned, but sure I am that we cannot grow fond of them without prejudice to devotion. The stags when they find themselves too fat hide in the thickets, knowing that being burdened with their own weight they would not be able to run, if they should be hunted. The heart of man, overcharged with unprofitable and perilous affections, cannot run after GOD readily, swiftly, and eagerly—which is the chief point of devotion.

Little children delight in catching butterflies, and none think ill of them, because they are little children; but is it not a ridiculous, nay rather, a lamentable thing to see men amuse and busy themselves with such unbecoming trifles as those which I have named? which, besides their unprofitableness put us in danger of committing faults and extravagances in their pursuit.

Wherefore, I say that we must be cleansed from these affections; for though the acts are not always contrary, yet the affections are always injurious, to true devotion.

CHAPTER XVI.

On regulating our Natural Inclinations.

WE have, let us observe, certain natural inclinations, which, not having sin for their origin, are not properly *sins*, but may be called imperfections, and their acts may be termed faults, or failings. For example S. Jerome tells us of a holy woman who had so great an inclination to grief and sadness that on the death of her children and her husband she well-nigh died of sorrow. This was an imperfection, not a sin; seeing that it was wholly contrary to her will.

There are some naturally light-hearted, others of sombre mind; some are averse to receiving advice, some inclined to indignation, some prone to anger others to love—in short, there are few persons in whom such imperfections may not be observed. Now, although these inclinations are natural, they may by care, and by nourishing the contrary affections, be corrected and moderated, if not wholly destroyed.

And this ought to be accomplished. Men have found means to change the bitter almond tree into a sweet one, simply by piercing it at the root, to let out the sap; why then may we not let out our evil inclinations, and become better?

There is no nature so good that it may not be corrupted by vicious habits; nor any so perverse that it may not, first by the Grace of God, and next by industry and diligence, be subdued and overcome.

I will now give you advice and propose the exercises by means of which you may disengage your soul from evil affections and from attachment to things useless and dangerous, and strengthen yourself against temptations to mortal sin.

God give you grace to practise them well.

PART THE SECOND.

CONTAINING INSTRUCTIONS FOR ELEVATING THE SOUL TO GOD BY PRAYER AND THE SACRAMENTS.

CHAPTER I.

Of the necessity of Prayer.

PRAYER places our understanding in the brightness of the light of GOD, and exposes our will to the warmth of heavenly love. There is nothing which so frees the mind from ignorance and the will from evil inclinations. It is the water of benediction which makes the plants of our good desires grow green and flourish, which washes the soul from its imperfection and quenches the passions of our hearts.

But above all I counsel mental prayer, and particularly that which centres round the life and passion of our LORD. In meditating often upon these, your soul will be filled with Him, and you will learn from His actions how to model your own. He is the Light of the World, and it is in Him, by Him, and for Him that we should be illumined and "shine as lights in the world." He is the Tree of our desires, the Shade of our refreshment, the Living Fountain of life in which we may wash away all our stains.

Children, from hearing their mothers and trying to prattle with them, learn in time to speak their language; so we, living near our SAVIOUR by meditation, and observing His words, His actions, His love, shall, by the help of His grace, learn to speak and act and will like Him. Here we must rest; and, believe me, we can find access to GOD the FATHER by no other Door; for as the glass of a mirror could not arrest our view, if it had not some metal at the back, so could not Divinity be contemplated by us in this lower world, were It not united with the sacred humanity of our SAVIOUR, Whose Life and Passion and Death are subjects of meditation best fitted to the feebleness of our sight, most sweet to our heart, most useful for the forming of our habits. It was not for nothing that our LORD called Himself "the Bread Which came down from Heaven;" for as bread can be eaten with every sort of food, so the SAVIOUR can and ought to be meditated upon and sought after, in all our prayers and actions.

In this spiritual exercise then employ one hour every day, before dinner, or if possible early in the morning, when your mind will be less distracted, and refreshed by the repose of the night. Do not take more than an hour, unless specially advised to do so.

If you could spend this hour in the church, it would be better for you and more convenient; because then neither father nor mother, wife nor husband, nor indeed any one, could rightly hinder you; whereas in your own home you could probably not have quiet and uninterrupted leisure.

Begin all your prayers, whether mental or vocal, by placing yourself in thought in the Presence of GOD. Hold strictly to this rule and you will see in a little time how good and profitable it is.

Pray always with your attention fixed, and your feelings roused to the sense of the words: pray ever from the heart; for believe me, the LORD's Prayer said with feeling and affection, is of infinitely more worth and value than ever so many or ever so long prayers said in haste and

If whilst praying vocally, you feel your heart drawn to mental prayer, refuse not the invitation, but let your mind turn gently, as it will; and be not concerned at not finishing that which you had begun, for the mental prayer you will thus offer to GOD will be more pleasing to Him, and more profitable to your own soul.

Should it happen that, through pressure of business or some accidental cause, your morning pass without allowing you leisure for the exercise of mental prayer, endeavour as soon as possible to repair the loss. But if the whole day pass and throughout it you find no time for this heavenly exercise, multiply your ejaculatory prayers and read some book of devotion, firmly resolving to overcome all obstacles to this sweet service on the morrow.

CHAPTER II.

A brief method of Meditation: and first, of the Presence of God which is the first point of preparation.

BUT perhaps you know not how to pray mentally, for it is a thing with which few in our age are so happy as to be acquainted. Here then I present you with a simple and short method, that by reading good books upon the subject, and above all by the practice of it, you may be amply instructed.

I will begin with the preparation, which consists in placing yourself in the Presence of GOD, and in imploring His assistance; and to aid you in the first of these points I will propose four principal means.

The first consists in a lively apprehension of GOD's Presence in all things and in every place; for there is neither place nor thing in all the world, where He is not most truly present; so that as birds whithersoever they fly meet with the air, so we, wheresoever we go, wheresoever we are, find our GOD encompassing us.

Every one acknowledges this truth, but few rightly realize it. Blind men, who see not their prince though present with them, behave nevertheless with respect, when they are told of his presence; but the truth is that seeing him not, they easily forget this and lose too readily their respect and reverence.

Alas! we do not see GOD, Who is present with us; and

though faith warns us of that Divine Ubiquity, yet seeing It not with our eyes we often forget It and act as though He were far from us; for though we well know that He is present in all things, yet not reflecting on it, we act as if we knew it not. This is why, before praying, you should always rouse in your soul a real apprehension of the Presence of GOD, such as David felt when he exclaimed, "If I climb up into heaven, Thou art there, if I go down to hell, Thou art there also." (Psalm cxxxix. 7.) And so we may use the words of Jacob, who, having beheld the sacred ladder, cried, "How dreadful is this place!" "Surely the LORD is in this place, and I knew it not," (Gen. xxviii. 17, 16), meaning that he had not thought upon it; for he could not be ignorant that GOD is everywhere. When, therefore, you come to prayer, you must say with all your heart, "Truly the LORD is here."

The second means of placing yourself in the Divine Presence is, to reflect that GOD is not only in the place where you are, but that He is, after a peculiar manner, in your heart and mind, which He quickens and animates, dwelling within you as the Heart of your heart, the Spirit of your spirit; for as the soul, diffused through the whole body, is in every part thereof, and yet dwells especially in the heart; even so GOD, being everywhere present, yet dwells in an especial manner in our spirit. It is for this reason that David calls Him *the Strength of his heart*, (Psalm lxxiii. 25); and St. Paul says that it is in GOD "we live, and move, and have our being." (Acts xvii. 28.) Reflecting upon this truth, you will feel more profound reverence towards GOD, Who is so intimately with you.

A third means is to think upon our SAVIOUR in His humanity, looking down from Heaven upon all mankind, particularly upon Christians, who are His children, most of all upon those who are at prayer. This is not mere imagination, but a real truth; for though we see Him not, as at his martyrdom S. Stephen saw Him, He from on high beholds us, and we may take into our mouth the words of the Sacred Spouse. "Behold, He standeth behind our wall, He looked forth at the windows, shewing Himself through the lattice." (Cant. ii. 9.)

The fourth means consists in representing, by our imagination, our LORD JESUS CHRIST in His sacred humanity, as if He were near to us—as we sometimes imagine some friend to be present and say, "I can see him now, doing this or that."

Use then some of these means of placing yourself in the Presence of GOD, before prayer; not all at once, but one at a time; and do it briefly and simply.

CHAPTER III.

Of Invocation, the second point of the preparation.

INVOCATION is made after this manner. The soul feeling itself in the Presence of GOD, prostrates itself in humblest reverence, acknowledging itself unworthy to come before Him; yet, knowing that this is His Will, it craves His Grace to serve and worship Him in this Meditation. You may, if you wish, use some short and heart-stirring words, like those of David, "Cast me not away from Thy Presence, and take not Thy HOLY SPIRIT from me." (Psalm li. 11.) "Give me understanding, and I shall keep Thy law; yea I shall keep it with my whole heart." "I am Thy servant, O grant me understanding, that I may know Thy testimonies." (Psalm cxix. 34, 125.)

CHAPTER IV.

Of the third point of preparation, which consists in proposing the Subject of the Mystery whereon we mean to meditate.

AFTER these two general points of the preparation, there remains a third which is not common to all meditations, and which some call "Fabrication du lieu;"* others the Inward Lesson. This is nothing less than to represent to your imagination the Mystery whereon you desire to meditate, as if it were really passing in your presence. For example, would you meditate on the Crucifixion of our LORD, imagine yourself to be on Mount Calvary, there to behold all that was done, to hear all that was said, on the day of the Passion; or, if you will, imagine that in the place where you are, the SAVIOUR is being crucified, as the Evangelists have described. The same rule is to be observed when you meditate on death (as I have indicated above) or hell, or any Mystery where things visible and

* I confess myself unable to give an English rendering of this phrase. It signifies the arranging of the subject in order, in one's mind; but I know of no words which will express this shortly, and prefer to leave the French as it stands.

sensible form part of the subject; but with reference to other Mysteries, such as the greatness of GOD, the excellence of Virtue, the end for which we are created, &c.—which are things invisible,—we cannot have the aid of our imagination. True, we might use some similitude or comparison, such as we see in the beautiful Parables of our LORD, to assist us in the consideration of them, but this is attended with considerable difficulty; and I only wish to instruct you in so plain and easy a method as that your spirit may not be wearied in the search for similes. By this means we confine our spirit within the mystery we wish to meditate on that it may not ramble to and fro; just as we encage a bird, or tie a hawk by her leash that she may rest on the hand.

Some will tell you that it is better to use the simple eye of faith, the simple apprehension of the spirit, in the representation of these mysteries; or else to imagine that the events are enacted in your own spirit; but this is too subtle for a beginner, and until GOD has raised you higher, I counsel you to remain in the lowly vale of piety I have shown to you.

CHAPTER V.

Of Considerations, which form the Second Part of the Meditation.

AFTER the exercise of the imagination follows that of the understanding — Meditation; which consists in framing one or more considerations in order to raise our affections to GOD and heavenly things. In this it is that meditation differs from studious thought or reflexion. The end of study is knowledge; the end and object of meditation is the love of GOD and the practice of virtue.

Having then encaged your spirit within the bounds of the subject on which you wish to meditate (either by the imagination if the matter be an object of sense, or by a simple proposal of it if it be not) begin to form considerations upon it, after the model I have set before you in the foregoing meditations; and if your mind find light and your spirit nourishment in any one of them, stop there: like the bees, who never quit the flower so long as they can suck honey from it. But if upon trial your spirit enter not with ease into this consideration, or your heart find in it no attraction, pass on to another with a calm and tranquil mind, not hastily or with labour.

CHAPTER VI.

Of Affections and Resolutions; the third part of the Meditation.

MEDITATION breathes into our will good and holy influences, such as the love of GOD and our neighbour, the desire of heavenly and eternal glory, zeal for the salvation of souls, the longing to imitate the Life of our LORD, compassion, admiration, joy; fear of GOD's wrath, of judgment and of hell; hatred of sin, confidence in the goodness and mercy of GOD and self-abasement for the sins of our past life; in all which affections the soul ought to be exercised.

But you must not stop at these general affections; you must pass from them to the forming of special and particular resolutions, for your progress in virtue. For eample, the first word of our SAVIOUR upon the cròss will kindle in your soul a desire to pardon and love your enemies; but this will be little worth, if you do not add to it a special resolution, after this manner, "I will no more be offended by the hard words of such an one, nor resent any affront he may offer me; but on the contrary, I will embrace every opportunity to win and soften him." By this means you will, with GOD's help, correct your faults in a little time, whereas by affections *only* you would find it a long and difficult task.

CHAPTER VII.

Of the Conclusion, and the Spiritual Bouquet.

LAST of all, we must conclude our meditation by making three Acts, which must be done with the utmost humility. First, by thanking GOD for the good affections and resolutions wherewith He has inspired us, and for His goodness and mercy revealed in the Mystery of the meditation.

The Life of Devotion.

Secondly, by ascribing to His Divine Majesty all the glory which can flow to Him from this exercise of His mercy, and all other His perfections, and by offering to Him our affections and resolutions, in union with the virtues of JESUS CHRIST His SON, and the Merits of His Death.

Thirdly, by asking GOD to communicate to us the graces and virtues of His SON, and to bless our affections and resolutions, that we may faithfully carry them into execution.

Then we pray for the Church, our Pastors, relations, friends, and others; concluding with the LORD's Prayer, which is the general and necessary prayer of all the faithful.

From all this, as I have already advised, gather a little bouquet of devotion. What I mean is this:—They who have been walking in a beautiful garden do not willingly leave it without gathering a few flowers to enjoy the sight and scent of during the whole day; so we, having refreshed our spirit by meditation on some mystery, ought to select one or two thoughts which we have found most to our mind, or which have most touched our heart, to ponder over during the course of the day. This, being done in the place where we have been meditating, will refresh us in our after solitude.

CHAPTER VIII.

Useful Advice upon the Practice of Meditation.

ABOVE all is it necessary, in rising from meditation, to remember the good resolutions you have made, in order carefully to practise them that very day. This is the great fruit of meditation, without which it is not only unprofitable, but often hurtful; because virtue meditated upon and not practised, will frequently puff up the mind, and make us believe ourselves to *be* such as we have resolved to become. If our resolutions are solid and real, it will doubtless in time be true of us, that we are what we have resolved to be; but if they are not, that is, if we take no pains to carry them into practice, they are vain and dangerous. We must therefore by all means endeavour to practise them, and seek every occasion, little or great, to do so. For example, if I have resolved to win, by gentleness, one who has offended me (or whom I have offended), I will seek this very day an opportunity to meet him, and greet him kindly; or, if I cannot meet him, at least to speak well of him and pray to GOD on his behalf.

After prayer be very careful to give yourself no mental shock, lest you scatter and dissipate the heavenly balm which you have received in meditation. My meaning is: it will be better for you to keep silence for a little while, if it be possible, and turn your mind gently from prayer to business, retaining as long as you can a feeling of the affections you have conceived. A man who has received in a vessel of fine porcelain some liquid of great price, in carrying it home walks gently, not looking from side to side, but generally before him, for fear of stumbling or making a false step, and sometimes upon the vessel for fear of spilling the liquid; even so ought you to act when your meditation is ended. Do not let anything distract you. If, for instance, you meet with anyone whom you are obliged to converse with, keep watch over your heart, that its holy affections be not squandered.

You must accustom yourself to pass from prayer to those occupations which your state of life requires, however different they may seem from the affections which you then received. Thus the advocate must learn to pass from prayer to pleading, the merchant to his traffic, the married woman to the duties of her household, with such ease and tranquillity that the mind be not disturbed; for since both occupations are in accordance with the Will of God, we must learn to move calmly from the one to the other in the spirit of humility and devotion.

It will sometimes happen, that immediately after preparation, your affections will be moved towards God. Give them the reins without trying to follow the method I have indicated; for though, generally speaking, the mental exercise will precede that of the spirit, yet if the Holy Ghost work in your soul holy affections during or even before the considerations, do not return to the latter; remembering that their only purpose is to excite in your heart holy desires. In short, whenever affections arise, open your heart to receive them. The same may be said with regard to the thanksgiving, oblation and petition—my object in arranging them in order, being merely to distinguish more plainly the parts of prayer. The resolutions, however, are always to be made after the affections, and at the end, before the conclusion of the whole meditation; because, as these have reference to familiar objects, they would earlier in the meditation distract the spirit, and draw it from the object of its desires.

In the affections and resolutions, it is well to use colloquy, and to speak sometimes to our LORD, sometimes to the angels and persons represented in the mystery; to the saints, to ourselves, to our own hearts;—after the manner of David in the Psalms, and of other saints in their prayers and meditations.

CHAPTER IX.

Of the Dryness which we sometimes feel in Meditation.

SHOULD it happen that you feel no pleasure or comfort in meditation, I pray you not to be troubled; speak aloud in prayer, lamenting before your LORD your coldness, confessing your unworthiness, and beseeching Him to assist you. Say to Him those words of Jacob, "I will not let Thee go, except Thou bless me" (Gen. xxxii. 26), or of the Canaanite woman, "Truth, LORD," I am a dog, "yet the dogs eat of the crumbs which fall from their master's table." (S. Matt. xv. 27.)

At another time take up some devotional book and read it with attention, till your spirit be aroused within you; or stir up your heart by some exterior posture of devotion, such as prostrating yourself on the ground, provided you are alone and in some private place. If, after this, you still receive no comfort, be not cast down, however great your dryness, but continue to kneel devoutly before GOD. How many courtiers go a hundred times a year into the prince's presence-chamber, without hope of speaking to him, but only to be seen of him and to pay their homage! So ought we to come to holy prayer, purely and simply to pay our homage and testify our fidelity to God; and should it please His Divine Majesty to speak to us, to breathe upon us holy desires and inward consolation, it will doubtless be to us an exceeding honour and most heart-stirring happiness. But if it should please Him not to grant us this favour, but to leave us, unregardful of our prayers or of our presence, we must not therefore go from Him; on the contrary, we should remain before His Sovereign Goodness with devotion and tranquillity of spirit; and then, observing our patience, our importunity and perseverance, He will, when again we come before Him, enrich us with His consolations, and make us to experience the sweetness of holy prayer. Yet if He should not do so, let us rest content that even this is an honour too great for us—to come before Him and be admitted into His Presence.

CHAPTER X.

Of the Morning Exercise.

BESIDES this mental prayer, and other vocal prayers which you ought to say once every day, there are five other shorter descriptions, which may be used as helps to these, and of which the first is the morning exercise, intended as a general preparation for the work of the day. Its method is as follows:

1. Thank and adore GOD with deep veneration, for having preserved you from the dangers of the past night; and if your conscience accuse you of sin, ask pardon of Him.

2. Consider that the day you are entering upon, is given you that you may advance towards the bright eternal day; and make a firm purpose to employ it to that end.

3. Forecast within yourself the business and occupations of the day; what occasions you may have of serving GOD; what temptations to offend Him, either by anger or vanity or any other wrong-doing. Prepare yourself with holy resolution, to employ well such means as may be given you

of doing GOD service, and of advancing in the devout life; and on the other hand arm yourself with the Panoply of GOD, to avoid, or to combat and conquer every foe to your own salvation and His glory. Do not think it sufficient, however, to make a good resolution, but prepare the means to execute it well. For example: if I foresee that I shall have to deal, in any business, with a passionate person—one quick to anger—I shall not only resolve to guard against giving him offence, but shall prepare words of meekness to ward off his wrath, or seek the assistance of some one who will command his forbearance. Or if I foresee that I shall have an opportunity of visiting some sick person, I shall arrange the hour, as well as the help and consolation I may be able to afford him. And so of the rest.

4. This done, humble yourself before GOD, acknowledging that of yourself you can carry out no resolve, whether it be to flee from evil, or to do good. And, holding, as it were, your heart in your hand, offer it together with all your good resolves, to His Divine Majesty, supplicating Him to take it into His protection and to enmighten it that it may daily proceed in all virtue and godliness.

Use these or the like words, "Behold, O LORD, this poor heart of mine, which by Thy bounty has conceived some good affections, but which, alas! is of itself too feeble and wretched to do the good it desires, unless Thou impart to it Thy heavenly blessing. This blessing I now implore, O FATHER of Mercies, through the merits of Thy SON, to Whose honour I consecrate this and all the remaining days of my life."

All these spiritual acts must be made briefly and fervently, before you leave your room, if possible; that, by means of this exercise, all you do throughout the day may be watered with the dew of GOD's benediction. And I pray you never to fail herein.

CHAPTER XI.

Of the Evening Exercise and Examination of Conscience.

As before your material dinner you have made a spiritual dinner by means of meditation, so in the evening you must

The Life of Devotion.

make a spiritual meal. Take then some little opportunity before supper, and prostrate before GOD, recall your spirit again to its true centre, JESUS CHRIST Crucified, Whom you will represent to yourself by a simple consideration; kindle again in your heart the fire of your morning's meditation, thinking over the points which most pleased you; or if you will, rouse yourself to devotion by some new subject.

As to the Examination of Conscience which must always be made before bedtime—every one knows how this is to be practised.

1. We give thanks to GOD for preserving us during the day past.

2. We examine our conduct through the several hours of the day; recalling where we have been and with whom, and also how we have been occupied.

3. If we find that we have done any good, we shall thank GOD for it; if, on the other hand, we have done evil, whether in thought, word or deed, we must ask pardon of His Divine Majesty, firmly resolving to amend.

4. And last, we commend to His Divine protection our-

self, our soul and body, the holy Church throughout the world, our relations, friends, and all for whom we desire to pray; and thus with the blessing of GOD we retire to the rest He has appointed for us.

This Exercise, like that of the morning, must *never* be forgotten. By that of the morning, the windows of the soul are opened to the light of Heaven; by this of the evening, they are closed to the darkness of hell.

CHAPTER XII.

Of the Spiritual Retreat.

IT is here that I wish you, with all affection, to follow my counsel, for in this subject consists one of the most assured means of spiritual advancement.

Recollect as often as you can during the day, by means of any of the four methods I have pointed out, that you should stand ever in the Presence of GOD: mark what He does, and what you are doing, and you will see His Eye fixed upon you with boundless love. O my GOD, you will say, why do I not alway raise my eyes to Thee, as Thou dost ever look upon me? Why thinkest Thou so often upon me, O LORD, and why think I so little upon Thee? Where art thou, O my soul? Our true Place to hide us in, is GOD; where do we now find ourselves?

As birds have their nests in the trees, to which, when need is, they can retreat; and the deer have bushes and thickets wherein to remain under covert and to enjoy the cool shade in the heat of summer, so should our hearts choose some place to which we may occasionally retire and refresh ourselves amidst our worldly business; and there, as in a stronghold, defend ourselves against temptation. Happy is he who can say with truth to our LORD, Thou art "my Stronghold, whereunto I may alway resort!" "my House of Defence and my Castle;" "my Refuge from the storm, my Shadow from the heat." (Psalm lxxi. 2. Isaiah xxv. 4.)

Remember then to make occasional retreats into the solitude of your own heart, whilst outwardly engaged in conversation or business. This mental solitude cannot be intruded upon by the company you may be in; for their outward intercourse with you touches not your heart which may, if it will, rest alone in the Presence of GOD.

This indeed was the practice of King David amid his various occupations, as is witnessed in these and a thousand other passages in the Psalms: "I am alway by Thee; for Thou hast holden me by my right hand. Unto Thee lift I up mine eyes, O Thou that dwellest in the heavens. Mine eyes are ever looking unto the LORD. I have set GOD always before me, &c." (Psalm lxxiii. 22, cxxiii. 1, xxv. 14, xvi. 9). Truly our occupations are seldom so engrossing but that we may from time to time withdraw our heart from them to enjoy this divine solitude. And to this I counsel you. Say with David, "I am become like a pelican in the wilderness, and like an owl that is in the desert. I have watched and am even as it were a sparrow that sitteth alone upon the housetop" (Psalm cii. 6. 7). Which words, besides their literal meaning—that this great king spent many solitary hours in contemplation of things spiritual—point, in a mystical sense, to three excellent retreats wherein we may imitate the loneliness of our SAVIOUR; Who on Mount Calvary was likened to the "pelican in the wilderness" feeding her young with her own life-blood; at His Nativity in the lowly manger, to the owl, mourning and weeping for our offences and sins; and in His Ascension, to the sparrow flying up to Heaven, which is, as it were, the "housetop" of the world.

So, to these three solitudes may we make our spiritual retreats, even amidst the turmoil of business: so in all the employments of life may we live near to the SAVIOUR.

CHAPTER XIII.

Of Aspirations, Ejaculatory Prayers and Good Thoughts.

WE retire into GOD, because we aspire to Him; we aspire to GOD, that we may retire into Him; so that the spiritual retreat and the aspiration of the heart to Him, are a mutual support; and both proceed from the same source, viz. devout and pious thoughts.

Wherefore lift the heart to GOD in fervent aspiration;

admire His perfections; invoke His help; cast yourself in spirit at the foot of the Cross; adore His infinite goodness; speak often to Him (for He will hear and answer); give your soul to Him, not once but many times a day; contemplate His clemency; stretch out your hand to Him as a little child to his father, that He may lead you on; plant Him in your soul like a Standard, under Which you will do battle with your enemies; in a word, arouse in your heart, by a thousand emotions, tender and devout love for your Divine LORD.

To this end S. Augustine strongly counsels ejaculatory prayer; for, by accustoming the spirit to hold frequent and close communion with GOD, it becomes suffused with the fragrance of His perfections. There is, moreover, no difficulty in this exercise; it may be mingled with our ordinary occupations, and rather helps forward than hinders our work. The traveller who takes a little wine to cheer and refresh him, though he may stay a moment on his journey to do so, hinders not his progress, but on the contrary acquires strength to go on his way with ease. He has tarried that he may the better speed.

The Life of Devotion.

Many have collected ejaculatory prayers—all, I doubt not, very useful; but I would counsel you not to confine yourself to any set form of words, but to give utterance either with the heart or lips to whatever love may prompt: for it will supply all you need. It is true, certain words have peculiar power to calm and satisfy the heart—such as the ejaculations scattered so freely throughout the Book of Psalms; the frequent invocation of the Name of JESUS; the breathings of divine Love in the Song of Songs. Spiritual songs will also answer the same purpose if sung with heart and feeling.

Spiritual collectedness, indeed, and ejaculatory prayers may supply the want of other prayers; but failing in them, the loss can scarcely be repaired by any other means. Without them we cannot lead a contemplative life and can ill perform the duties of an active one. Without them repose is but idleness, and labour vexation.

Wherefore I conjure you, to practise these with all your heart.

CHAPTER XIV.

How we ought to hear and read the Word of God.

LISTEN devoutly to the Word of GOD, whether you read it, or hear it in religious conversation with your friends, or in sermons. Receive it with reverence; let it not fall to the ground unheeded, but take it as a precious balm to your heart—imitating the example of the Blessed Virgin, who pondered in her heart all the words of her Divine SON. And remember that our LORD gathers up the words we address to Him in our prayers, after the measure in which we receive those He speaks to us.

Have always at hand some good devotional book—such as the Spiritual Combat, the Confessions of S. Augustine, the Epistles of S. Jerome and other similar books—and read every day a little, with as great earnestness and attention as if you were reading a letter which these saints had sent from heaven to show you the way, and encourage you to walk in it. Read also the histories and lives of holy men and women, in which as in a looking-glass you may see the true portraiture of a Christian life, and suit their actions to your own state; for, although many of the acts of the saints cannot absolutely be imitated by those living in the world, yet all may be in some degree followed.

CHAPTER XV.

Of Frequent Communion.

It is said that Mithridates, King of Pontus, having invented mithridate,* so strengthened his body thereby, that afterwards, when he would have poisoned himself to escape falling into the hands of the Romans, he could not. The Saviour has instituted the august Sacrament of the Eucharist, in which we verily and indeed partake of His Body and Blood, to the end that whoso eateth thereof may live for ever. He therefore who comes often and with devotion to the Holy Communion, so confirms the health of his soul, that it is almost impossible he should be

* An antidote against poison.

poisoned by any kind of evil affection. One cannot be nourished with this Bread of Life, and at the same time live to dead affections.

Just as man, dwelling in the earthly Paradise, might have avoided the death of the body by feeding on the fruit of the Tree of Life which GOD had planted therein; so may we also avoid the death of the soul by feeding on this Sacrament of life. If the most tender fruits, and such as are most subject to corruption, can be easily preserved through the year with sugar or honey, it is no marvel if our hearts, however frail and feeble, be preserved from the corruption of sin, when sweetened with the incorruptible Flesh and Blood of the SON of GOD. Believe me, Christians who are finally reprobate will be without reply when the just Judge shall upbraid them with their madness in choosing *death*, when life and health were set before them, so easily to be preserved by the means which CHRIST Himself has left us. Wretched ones, will He say, Why did ye die, having the food of Life ever within your reach?

"I neither praise nor blame the practice of receiving the Holy Communion every day (says S. Augustine), but I counsel and exhort each one to communicate every Sunday, provided his soul be free from affection for sin."

With the same holy Doctor of the Church, I neither approve nor condemn daily communion. The disposition required for this practice must be so *perfect*, that it is not prudent to recommend it generally ; and yet so excellent a spirit is to be found in some, that it is not good to dissuade universally : it is indeed a practice to be regulated by the consideration of the spiritual state of each individual, and never to be adopted save with the advice and sanction of the "spiritual Pastor."

But you see that S. Augustine strongly exhorts us to communicate every Sunday; follow then his advice as far as you may be able, if, as I am supposing, you have no affection for mortal or venial sin, and are in the disposition which S. Augustine requires.

Many lawful hindrances may however occur, not perhaps on your own part, but through those with whom you live. If, for example, you are in any sort of subjection, and those to whom you owe duty and reverence are so ill instructed or so capricious as to be disquieted by seeing you communicate often; will it not be wise, all things considered, to condescend in some measure to their infirmity, and to communicate—say once a fortnight:—but this, only in case you can by no means overcome the difficulty.

As a general rule cannot be laid down in this matter, we must act according to the counsel of our spiritual adviser: but I can say with confidence, we must never communicate less frequently than once a month, if we desire to serve GOD devoutly.

If you are prudent, neither father nor mother, wife nor husband, will prevent you from communicating often; for since, on the day of your communion you will be careful to neglect no duty, and will even be more cheerfully active in showing kindness to them, and in obeying their wishes however irksome, it is not probable that they will seek to debar you from an exercise which causes them no inconvenience: unless indeed they are of very froward and unreasonable disposition; and in this case I have advised that you yield somewhat to their wishes.

CHAPTER XVI.

How we ought to Communicate.

BEGIN to prepare for Holy Communion the evening before, using many aspirations of the soul to GOD, many ejaculations of love to Him, and retiring to rest a little earlier than usual, that you may earlier rise. If you wake in the night, fill your heart with thoughts of JESUS, Who in your sleep watches over you and prepares for you a thousand favours, if you be willing to receive them. In the morning rise with alacrity to enjoy the happiness you hope for, and, confessing your sins, go with great confidence and yet greater humility, to receive this heavenly food which nourishes your soul to immortality; having received It, rouse your heart to do homage to the great King of your Salvation, speak to Him in prayer, think of Him as taking up His abode in your heart; and so conduct yourself that it may be plain to all men that GOD is with you of a truth.

If you cannot enjoy Sacramental Communion, you may at least Communicate spiritually and unite yourself with CHRIST by earnest and loving desire for His life-giving Flesh and Blood.*

Your chief intention in communicating ought to be to advance, comfort and strengthen yourself in the love of GOD; for you must receive by love that which Love giveth to you. We cannot conceive of our SAVIOUR in any action more full of love and tenderness than this in which He gives Himself to us, that He may penetrate our souls and

---

* "But if a man, either by reason of extremity of sickness, or for want of warning in due time to the Curate, or for lack of company to receive with him, or by any other just impediment, do not receive the Sacrament of CHRIST's Body and Blood, the Curate shall instruct him, that if he do truly repent him of his sins and stedfastly believe that JESUS CHRIST hath suffered death upon the Cross for him, and shed His Blood for his redemption, earnestly remembering the benefits he hath thereby, and giving Him hearty thanks therefor, he doth eat and drink the Body and Blood of our SAVIOUR CHRIST profitably to his soul's health, though he do not receive the Sacrament with his mouth."

Rubric in the Office for the Communion of the Sick.

unite Himself intimately to the hearts of His faithful ones.

If the worldly ask you why you communicate so often, tell them it is because you would learn to love GOD, would be purified from your imperfections, be delivered from your troubles, be comforted in your affliction, be supported in your weakness. Tell them that two classes of people ought to communicate frequently: the *perfect*, because being well-disposed, they would be very wrong not to draw near to the Source and Fountain of perfection, and the *imperfect*, that they may be able to aspire to the perfect life; the *strong*, lest they become weak, and the *weak* that they may grow strong; the *sick*, that they may be restored to health, and the *healthy*, lest they fall into sickness; that for your part, being imperfect and weak and sick, you have need often to communicate with Him Who is the Source of perfection, of strength and healing.

Tell them, that they who have not much worldly business ought to communicate often because they have leisure, and they who are much occupied in worldly matters, because they especially need spiritual nourishment—as those who labour hard and are full of anxiety have need of solid food, and that frequently. Tell them, that you receive the Holy Sacrament that you may learn to receive it worthily; for no action which we perform seldom, can we perform well.

Wherefore communicate often—once every week if you can; and remember that as hares in the northern mountains become white in winter, because they neither see nor eat anything but snow, so by beholding and partaking of the beauty and purity and goodness of Him Who gives Himself to you in the Blessed Eucharist, you may become fair and pure and good, and daily grow more like to Him in all things.

THE END.

www.ingramcontent.com/pod-product-compliance
Lightning Source LLC
Chambersburg PA
CBHW032241080426
42735CB00008B/954